WOOLLY MAMMOTH

Life, Death, and Rediscovery

WOOLLY MAMMOTH

Life, Death, and Rediscovery

Windsor Chorlton

Library of Congress Cataloging-in-Publication Data is available.

ISBN 0-439-24134-0

10 9 8 7 6 5 4 3 2 1   01 02 03 04 05

Printed in Mexico   49
First printing, April 2001

 Produced by Miles Kelly Publishing Ltd
Bardfield Centre, Great Bardfield, Essex, CM7 4SL, U.K.

Additional text: Steve Parker

Project Manager: Anne Marshall
Designer: Jo Brewer
Copy Editor: Eleanor van Zandt
Proofreader and Indexer: Jane Parker
Picture Research: Lesley Cartlidge
Publishing Director: Jim Miles

Color reproduction: DPI Colour,
Saffron Walden, Essex, U.K.

Mammoth illustrations: Mike Saunders
Maps: Martin Sanders

Picture Credits
All photographs by Francis Latreille
except p11 T, Wolfgang Kaehler/Corbis
p11 B, Drac Rhône-Alpes
p15 T, Natural History Museum, U.K.
p15 B, Novosti
p35, Ryan Hockley
p36 TR, Murdo McLeod

All other pictures from the Miles Kelly archives.

KEY TO ABBREVIATIONS		
	t	= metric ton
cm = centimeter	ft	= feet
cm² = square centimeter	mi	= miles
km = kilometer	lb	= pound
l = liter	F	= Fahrenheit
m = meter	C	= Celsius

Contents

Foreword

The 1999 excavation and airlift of the Jarkov mammoth from the permafrost and ice of the Taimyr Peninsula of Siberia was a scientific "first." For the first time, the remains of a frozen woolly mammoth were removed from the tundra in a 26-ton (23.4-t) block and airlifted to the city of Khatanga, where the block containing the remains was placed in a permafrost cave. There, it will be studied in many ways, to find out all we can about this mammoth and the conditions in which it lived and died. Information from the Jarkov mammoth as well as from other frozen animals may help us to learn how mammoths and other Ice Age animals became extinct.

We will try to learn all we can about mammoths and where they lived, and why they died. It is like being a detective, using really old clues—Ice Age clues—to decide what caused their death. Was it natural? Or was it caused by overhunting?

Being able to participate in the Jarkov mammoth expedition was a chance of a lifetime. It was the first time I ever had a chance to "pet a mammoth" whose hair was still attached to its body. The mammoth, the tundra, the Dolgan people, the reindeer, the Russians, and the expedition team made it a very exciting and memorable experience.

Larry D. Agenbroad, PhD
Professor of Geology
Northern Arizona University
July 2000

Life on the frozen tundra

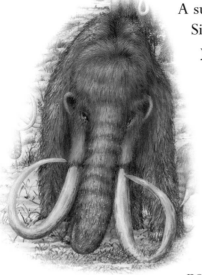

A summer day on the Siberian tundra, 20,000 years ago. The herd of woolly mammoths migrating north across the patchwork of snow and meadow stood out sharply in the clear arctic light. They moved slowly, feeding as they went. The youngsters grazed on the tender new grass and herbs, but the adults sometimes foraged for willow shoots sprouting beneath the melting snow patches. To reach the vegetation, they swung their great heads from side to side, using their 6-ft (1.8-m) curved tusks to sweep the ground clear of snow.

At this time of year, when the vegetation was at its most lush, the adult mammoths ate as much as 400 lb (180 kg) of food a day. They were building up fat reserves for the winter months. By the end of August, the ground would be frozen hard, and the mammoths would have started migrating southward. They spent their entire lives searching for food.

There were 20 mammoths in the herd—all females or young males. The adult bulls, traveling alone or in groups of two or three, kept pace with the herd at a distance. Occasionally, the males sparred among themselves, clashing tusks and butting their massive heads together. Summer was also the mammoth breeding season. The young, who spent 22 months in the womb, were born at the beginning of the spring growing season, nearly two years later.

Some of the adult males were huge, 11 ft (3.3 m) at the shoulder and weighing 7 tons (6.3 t). But they weren't the largest mammoths that ever lived. Their extinct ancestor, the mighty steppe mammoth, reached the impressive height of 15 ft (4.6 m) and weighed more than 13.5 tons (12.2 t)—the weight of 160 adult humans.

The mammoth herd in Siberia was well protected against the cold. Their bulky but compact bodies, small ears, and stubby tails were designed to conserve heat. As they moved across the tundra, the 3-ft-(90-cm) long fringe of coarse hair on their flanks swung like skirts.

As the herd grazed, their leader—an old female—kept alert for danger. From time to time, she spread her ears and raised her trunk, testing the air for threatening sounds or scents. The mammoths weren't the only creatures enjoying the arctic summer's brief bounty. On a low rise about 1 mi (1.6 km) away, three woolly rhinoceroses were grazing. In the bottom of the river valley, a pair of giant elk, with antlers 9 ft (2.7 m) across, browsed on a thicket of birches. On the other side of the river, a herd of musk oxen grazed on the tundra. Far downstream, reindeer converged in shallow water to drink.

All these animals attracted predators—wolves and lions, and

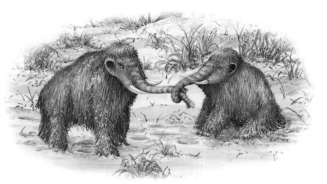

even saber-toothed cats that could disembowel a mammoth calf with one terrible slash of their razor-sharp canines. Although these hunters sometimes managed to pick off young or sickly mammoths, they rarely attacked a full-grown mammoth. At the first sign of danger, the herd formed a living fortress around the calves. A mammoth could snap a lion's spine with a blow of its trunk or a sideways swipe with its tusks.

The predator that mammoths feared most lived hundreds of miles to the south. Humans who had learned to combat the bitter winters with fire, animal furs, and shelters had discovered the mammoths' migration routes. Each year as the herds passed north or south, the hunters lay in wait.

Tackling a full-grown mammoth was a perilous activity, but stone spear tips found among mammoth skeletons show that hunters did prey on the biggest of all Ice Age game. Humans may have slaughtered whole herds of mammoths by forcing them to stampede over cliffs or driving them with fire into pitfalls. Mammoth flesh and fur provided food and clothing, while their bones and tusks were used for tools, weapons, statues, jewelry, and building materials.

A frantic trumpeting startled the mammoth herd. Their ears flared. One of the distant bull mammoths was in distress. The herd leader rolled back her trunk and blared a response, then set off toward the sound at a stiff-legged run. The rest of the herd lumbered after her, making the ground tremble under their weight. The trumpeting grew louder.

The mammoths rose over the crest and saw a terrible sight. One of the bulls had broken through the tundra into a hole created by the melting of a large mass of buried ice. Only his

head was aboveground. Despite the bull's strength, his struggles only mired him deeper in the ice and mud. The herd leader recognized the trapped mammoth. He had fathered several of her calves. She tried to reach him but was forced to retreat when the ground began to give way beneath her. Even if she could have reached him, there was nothing she could have done to save him.

For a day and a night, the herd remained by the doomed mammoth. His struggles grew weaker and weaker. On the morning of the second day, they stopped altogether. A few hours later, his corpse had sunk completely out of sight. The herd, uneasy, stayed near the grave for several hours longer and then left, dwindling to black specks on the plain, their bellows slowly fading into silence.

Thousands of years passed. The Ice Age ended. As the glaciers melted, the mammoths and many of the other large mammals that shared their world vanished from the face of the earth. In Siberia, nomadic tribes began to herd reindeer as well as hunt them. In the warmer regions, people took up farming and built towns. Empires rose and fell. All during this long span of history, the mammoth remained entombed in the Siberian ice. And there he would be lying still but for a chance encounter in 1997, when a young nomad boy spotted one of his tusks sticking out of the still-frozen tundra.

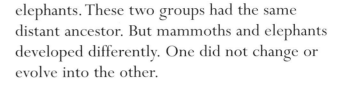

Age of the mammoths

Jarkov was a woolly mammoth. His long, shaggy fur kept out the bitter cold of the Ice Age in the far north. But there have been other kinds of mammoths during the past few million years. As they spread around the world, ice ages came and went. Animals and plants changed. Each type of mammoth became suited, or adapted, to its own surroundings.

The first mammoths

The first mammoth group probably began in Africa 4–5 million years ago. These mammoths were similar to their close cousins, the elephants. These two groups had the same distant ancestor. But mammoths and elephants developed differently. One did not change or evolve into the other.

Mammoths on the move

Some of the early mammoths spread from Africa into Central Europe. They evolved over one or two million years into the ancestral mammoth. In Europe and Asia this evolution continued over another million years to produce the greatest mammoth of all—the steppe mammoth. It had the beginnings of a furry coat, since the north was colder than Africa, and the creature had to

Ancestral (southern) mammoth
Mammuthus meridionalis
- Height 14 ft (4.3 m)
- Weight 9–11.5 tons (8.1–10.4 t)
- Appeared about 2–1.5 million years ago, probably in Central Europe
- No woolly coat
- Spread across Europe and Asia
- Moved east into North America by 1 million years ago

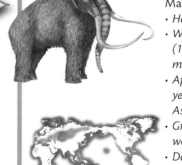

Steppe mammoth
Mammuthus trogontherii
- Height 15 ft (4.6 m)
- Weight 11.5–13.5 tons (10.4–12.2 t) (the biggest mammoth)
- Appeared by 600,000 years ago in Europe or Asia
- Gradually evolved a short, woolly coat
- Descended from ancestral mammoth
- Spread across Europe, Asia

Columbian (American) mammoth
Mammuthus columbi
- Height 13 ft (4 m) or more
- Weight 9–11.5 tons (8.1–10.4 t)
- Appeared by 100,000 years ago in North America, lived only here
- No woolly coat
- Descended from ancestral mammoth
- Spread as far south as present-day Mexico

Woolly mammoth
Mammuthus primigenius
- Height 11 ft (3.3 m)
- Weight 4.5–9 tons (4–8.1 t)
- Appeared about 250,000 years ago in Asia and Central Europe
- Long, shaggy coat
- Descended from steppe mammoth
- Moved east into North America by 100,000 years ago

retain body warmth. Also, the great ice ages were just beginning.

Steppe mammoths lived on the steppes—rolling grasslands with scattered trees, bushes, and shrubs. As the ice ages began in earnest, some steppe mammoths evolved smaller bodies and longer, hairy coats. They became a third type of mammoth, the woolly mammoth.

Mammoths head east

Meanwhile some ancestral mammoths had wandered from Siberia, in eastern Asia, to Alaska. Today this route is the Bering Strait, covered by sea. But during the ice ages, sea levels fell several times, and it was dry land for thousands of years at a time. Mammoths and other animals could walk across. Mammoths also spread from the continent of Europe to Britain when the English Channel was dry land.

Mammoths in the Americas

In North America the ancestral mammoths spread south and east. Gradually they evolved into Columbian mammoths. Later, woolly

Wrangel Island in the Arctic Ocean, off northeastern Siberia, is a treeless environment, isolated from the mainland. Mammoths survived here longer than anywhere else on Earth to less than 9,000 years ago.

mammoths from Asia also crossed the Bering Land Bridge. As the ice spread, it pushed plants and animals southward. Then the ice retreated and the habitats and their wildlife flourished. This is why woolly mammoth remains occur as far south as South Dakota.

For a time, North America had two kinds of mammoths. However, by about 12,000 years ago in Europe, and 10,000 years ago in North America, they were almost all gone.

Why did woolly mammoths disappear?

No one knows, but there are lots of different theories. The world was altering quickly 20,000–10,000 years ago. The last ice age faded rapidly—a type of natural global warming. The climate change brought many different plants and animals. Perhaps mammoths could not cope with these new plant foods and predators.

Another idea is that mammoths may have caught a terrible new kind of disease. Or an existing disease became more serious in the warmer conditions.

Possibly, ancient people hunted mammoths to extinction with spears, traps, axes, and other weapons. Pictures on Stone Age cave walls show lots of hunts.

Perhaps all these factors combined to bring about the extinction of the mammoths.

Mammoths are depicted in the paintings and engravings that decorate the walls of this cave in France.

Woolly mammoths

Have you ever been close to a real, live, full-grown elephant? It towers high above, its massive head looming way over yours. Its trunk can curl around you and lift you up like a donut. Its gigantic weight could squash you underfoot. Its tusks are longer than the length of your bed. Now imagine a creature that's as tall and strong. It has longer, more curved tusks, a huge humped back, and long, stringy hair all over. It's a great, shaggy mountain of muscle—a woolly mammoth. This vast beast was as big as any elephant today. It looked fierce and frightening. But, like the elephant, it was probably a peaceful plant eater. Until, that is, another animal got in its way or threatened its baby. Then it got annoyed.

Skeleton
The mammoth's thick bones supported its vast bulk. The huge skull was one-fifth of the weight of the whole skeleton.

Mammoth facts
Ordinary name: Woolly mammoth
Scientific name: *Mammuthus primigenius*
Weight: Females (cows) 4.5–5.5 tons (4–5 t), males (bulls) 6.75–9 tons (6.1–8.1 t)
Height: 9–11 ft (2.7–3.3 m) at the shoulder
Length: 15–18 ft (4.6–5.5 m) head and body, trunk about $6^1/_2$ ft (2 m), tail $3^1/_4$ ft (1 m)
Tusk size: $6^1/_2$–8 ft (2–2.5 m) around the curve in females, nearly 10 ft (3 m) in males; weight up to 187 lb (85 kg)
Gestation (pregnancy): 22 months
Size at birth: Height $3^1/_4$ ft (1 m), weight 220 lb (100 kg)
Life span: 70–80 years (if lucky)

Furry coat
The hairs of the mammoth's woolly coat were up to 3 ft (1 m) long. They were longest around the lower body and legs, like a dangling fringe. On the upper body the hairs were shorter, about 12 in (30 cm). But this was only the mammoth's outer "overcoat." Close to its skin was the "undercoat," a layer of shorter, thinner hairs packed closely together. These formed a 3-in-(8-cm) deep layer like a thick, warm, wraparound rug.

Tusks
A mammoth's two tusks were its enormous upper incisor teeth. Over about 20 years they grew out of the jawbone and beyond the lips, growing longer in males than in females. Tusks were used to sweep snow aside, to dig in the soil to find food, and to fight enemies like wolves. Male mammoths showed off their tusks and "fenced" with rival males at breeding time.

Trunk
The trunk was the mammoth's very long, very flexible, and very sensitive nose and upper lip. It grasped leaves and other foods from low on the ground or high in trees and passed them to its mouth. It also sucked up water to squirt into the mouth when drinking. It sniffed the air for scents. Also, it stroked family relatives and other herd members.

Feet
Each of the mammoth's feet had to support the weight of three small family cars. The foot was wide and flat, with an area about as big as four dinner plates. It was like an enormous snowshoe that distributed the mammoth's weight, so the great creature did not sink into soft soil, boggy marsh, or fresh snow. The rough skin on the sole of the foot could also grip, so that the mammoth did not slide on slippery ice.

Body hump

The woolly mammoth had a large hump on its shoulders and back. This was body fat. The fat acted as a store of food. It built up during the short warm season as the mammoth ate well. It was gradually used up during the long winter, when food was scarce and the mammoth went hungry.

Ears

The woolly mammoth's ears were small and furry, compared to those of an elephant. This helped to save body warmth. In bitter cold, large body extremities such as big ears or a long tail would get frostbitten, turn black, and fall off!

A large, full-grown woolly mammoth weighed about the same as:
2 large killer whales
4 white rhinos
12 small family cars
130 adult people
230 ten-year-old children

Mammoth finds

You are unlikely to find a deep-frozen mammoth at school or at work. But that's what happens in cold, icy Siberia. People go out to hunt, herd reindeer, lay cross-country pipelines, mine coal, dig for gold, or drill for oil. Probably several times each year, somewhere in the icy expanse, a person comes across preserved mammoth remains—usually by accident. Some remains are badly damaged and worth little. Others are more complete and well preserved, and could be worth millions of dollars.

The Beresovka mammoth

One of the largest and best-studied mammoths was a male about 40 years old, frozen for 30,000 years in the bank of the Beresovka River, in eastern Siberia. In 1901, an expedition led by Eugen Pfizenmayer and Otto Hertz left St. Petersburg. Their reports tell of the discomforts, difficulties, and dangers of mammoth expeditions. The members endured a four-month journey by train, cart, boat, horseback, reindeer sled, and foot over rough country to the remote, windy, frozen site. The mammoth rotted and stank as parts were thawed to be cut up. It took a month for the cold, exhausted workers to slice the great carcass into 27 chunks. Temperatures fell as low as −58°F (−50°C). After 10 months, the Beresovka mammoth arrived back in St. Petersburg, where it is still on display.

The left foreleg was still bent as if the animal had attempted to pull itself out of its perilous position.

How old were woolly mammoths?

People have probably been finding frozen woolly mammoth remains thawing out of the ice in the far north for thousands of years. They sold the tusks or carved tools and trinkets from them, and fed their dogs on the meat.

Because of the way the ice ages came and went, most of the frozen woolly mammoths in Siberia date from two main periods: 100,000–30,000 and 14,000–10,000 years ago. Jarkov is very unusual because he lived about 20,000 years ago.

The first museum mammoth

Scientists started to record frozen woolly mammoth remains from about 1750. Since then there have been about 20 worthwhile finds—almost all in Siberia.

One of the earliest was in 1799. This was found by a hunter at the mouth of the Lena River, far to the north of Yakutsk. Parts of it thawed and were eaten by wolves and other predators. Mikhail Adams, from the Russian Academy of Sciences in St. Petersburg, heard about the discovery and examined the remains in 1806. He brought back most of the skeleton, tusks, and plenty of skin and hair. This was the first woolly mammoth skeleton put back together and displayed in a museum, in St. Petersburg in 1808.

More frozen finds

In 1901, the same year as the Beresovka discovery (*see left*), a small male mammoth only 8 ft (2.4 m) tall was found on Siberia's Liakhov Islands. In 1914, it was sent to Paris for French scientists to study and display its skeleton. However, soon after this, Russia decided to keep all of its mammoth finds. The Liakhov mammoth is the only true Siberian mammoth that can be seen in another country.

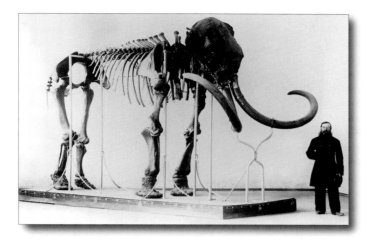

The Adams mammoth skeleton was complete except for one foreleg. Hair and skin were also found.

The "original" mammoth

In 1948, a frozen adult male mammoth was found on Siberia's Taimyr Peninsula. It was estimated to have died at about the age of 55—quite old for a woolly mammoth. It had only been in the ice for 11,500 years. Its skeleton was so complete that in 1990 it was chosen as the woolly mammoth "type specimen"—the most typical member of a species. All other mammoth finds are compared with it, to judge whether they are really woolly mammoths.

One of the mammoths frozen for the longest time, 43,000 years, was discovered near the Shandrin River of Siberia in 1972. Parts of its stomach and guts were preserved with almost 660 lb (300 kg) of food from its last meals. This is partly how we know what mammoths ate.

Recent finds

Perhaps the most famous and saddest find was Baby Dima in 1977 (*see below*). The same year two other discoveries were made in Siberia. One was a young female, about 12 years old when she died, near the Yuribei River on the Gydanskij Peninsula. The other was an adult male, the Khatanga mammoth, found by a reindeer herder near the Bolshaya Rassokha River.

Parts of Alaska have deep-freeze conditions similar to those of Siberia. They also have plenty of mammoth remains, which thaw regularly from the ice. But these are mainly bones, tusks, and teeth. Finds of hair, skin, and flesh are rare.

In 1988 another mammoth calf, called Mascha, was found in Siberia. She was probably only about three months old when she died near an offshoot of the Ob River on the Yamal Peninsula. Her body was more mummified, or dried, than frozen.

Then, in 1997, came Jarkov....

Baby Dima

Named after a local stream, Dima was found in 1977 by a gold mine's bulldozer driver, who was working along a small offshoot of the Berelekh River, in Siberia's Magadan region. Dima was about six months old and just 37 1/2 in (95 cm) tall when he died, some 40,000 years ago. His tusks had not yet grown beyond his lips, and his "baby teeth" were only slightly worn. So he had started to chew grass but still fed mainly on his mother's milk. Dima's body was thin and unhealthy, and after death some of its moisture was sucked out into the surroundings. This helped preservation and made Dima look even thinner and more shriveled—an "ice mummy." Like many of Siberia's preserved woolly mammoths, Dima was

probably not "quick frozen." He may have slipped and fallen into a grave such as a pond, bog, marshy mud, or quicksand. The cold conditions stopped his body from rotting until the whole area eventually froze.

Finding Jarkov

In 1997, reindeer herders of the nomadic Dolgan tribe discovered a pair of woolly mammoth tusks buried in Siberia's frozen tundra. When the French explorer Bernard Buigues heard of this, he persuaded the Dolgans to show him where they had found the tusks.

Buigues dug down through the permafrost and recovered the mammoth's head—still partly covered in hair. Convinced that the rest of the carcass lay preserved deep in the permafrost, Buigues spent a year putting together an expedition to remove it. His efforts paid off in September 1999, when an international team flew to the remote arctic site and began the task of digging out the mammoth.

After many problems and delays, the team freed the mammoth, together with the block of permafrost that enclosed it. The entire mass, weighing more than 26 tons (23.4 t), was airlifted by helicopter to the town of Khatanga and installed in a permafrost ice cave.

News of the "perfectly preserved" mammoth prompted speculation that DNA extracted from its cells could be used to create a living woolly mammoth. Most scientists think the chances of that are very slim. But researchers are excited at the opportunity to examine a mammoth preserved in the same condition as on the day it died. Jarkov, as he has been called, could tell us more about woolly mammoths and their Ice Age habitat. And he might also provide clues to the causes of their extinction.

An aerial view of the Jarkov excavation camp site showing the domed sleeping tents, the ridged mess tent, and the mammoth pit. The map shows the Taimyr Peninsula where Jarkov was found and Khatanga, the site of the ice cave.

Diary of the expedition

Summer 1997—The discovery

In the summer of 1997, nine-year-old Simion Jarkov went to visit his relatives 200 mi (320 km) northwest of Khatanga, a remote Siberian town on the Taimyr Peninsula. Simion is a Dolgan, one of a tribe of nomadic reindeer hunters and herders. One day, when Simion was out with the herd, he spotted the tip of a mammoth tusk poking out of the swampy tundra near the Balakhyna River. For Simion, this was like stumbling on buried treasure. With mammoth ivory worth around $50 a pound ($110 a kilogram), a tusk can fetch $5,000—more than the average Siberian worker earns in a year.

The Dolgans have used mammoth ivory for centuries, carving it into buttons, fishhooks, and ornaments. But as Simion scrambled to uncover more of the gleaming tusk, he was a little nervous. Among the Dolgans and other Siberian tribes, there is a widespread belief that mammoths are giant burrowing rodents that live underground and die when exposed to light. As creatures of the underworld, they are associated with death. According to superstition, bad luck and illness will strike anyone who interferes with their remains.

Dolgan reindeer herder Gennadi Jarkov shows off a piece of fur from the woolly mammoth that now bears his name. It was Gennadi and his younger brother, Simion, who discovered the mammoth in 1997.

Twenty thousand years after they were buried, Jarkov's tusks rise from the frozen tundra. The tip of the left tusk was probably damaged when Jarkov was alive, snapped off during a sparring session with another male mammoth.

A group of Dolgans look on admiringly as Jarkov's tusks are carried into the reindeer herders' settlement. Each tusk is more than 9 ft (2.7 m) long and weighs about 100 lb (45 kg).

Simion fetched his older brother, Gennadi. They succeeded in removing two well-preserved tusks. Measuring 9½ ft (2.9 m) long and weighing 100 lb (45 kg) each, the tusks were worth a small fortune.

The Jarkovs took the tusks to Khatanga to sell. That might have been the end of the story if news of their find hadn't reached Bernard Buigues, a French explorer and polar expedition guide who has spent nearly 10 years traveling in Siberia.

Buigues was interested in the tusks, but he was even more intrigued by the animal to which they had been attached. From the Jarkovs' description, it sounded as if at least part of the mammoth's frozen body was still in the ground. He persuaded the brothers to take him to the site. They were worried about his disturbing the mammoth's resting place. To avoid a curse, they told him, he should place money and a sacrificed white dog in the grave.

After the Jarkov brothers dug the tusks out of the tundra, they loaded them onto a reindeer sledge and carried them back to their settlement. The Jarkovs planned to sell the tusks to Siberian ivory traders.

Reindeer hunters of Siberia

The Jarkov brothers who found the woolly mammoth belong to a Siberian tribe called the Dolgans. The Dolgans settled on the Taimyr Peninsula in the 1600s and today number fewer than 7,000 people. Many of them are nomadic reindeer farmers and hunters.

The Dolgans hunt wild reindeer for food and use domesticated ones to haul their sledges. A Dolgan family may eat as many as three reindeer a month. They use the skins for clothing and as a covering for their traditional wood-framed tents and *balloks*—huts on runners pulled by reindeer.

The Dolgans also catch lots of fish, which they usually eat raw, and hunt ptarmigan (a kind of bird), wildfowl, and arctic fox. They sell fox fur and boil and eat the flesh. They used to kill and eat the meat of wolves, which they thought protected them from diseases.

Bernard Buigues examines Jarkov's jaw, which he dug up in 1998. The two giant molars in one jawbone clearly show the ridges used to chew tough grasses.

1998—An ambitious idea

In April 1998, Buigues began digging down through the rock-hard permafrost. It took him three days to reach the mammoth's head. The brain and other soft tissues had thawed and rotted away, but part of the fur had been preserved intact. Near the lower jaw, Buigues even found the red petals of a flower that had bloomed when mammoths still roamed the tundra. When he dried the sodden fur with a hair dryer, he discovered that the hair was thick and strong, ranging in texture from wiry to woolly, and with shades of color that varied from black to blond. He could even smell its pungent odor.

An ambitious idea began to form in Buigues's mind. What if the whole carcass could be removed? The rest of the deeply buried body would be better preserved than the head. There was even a possibility that its flesh and internal organs might be intact. No one had ever before succeeded in recovering a complete adult mammoth. Even the famous Beresovka specimen (see page 14) discovered in 1901 had been cut into more than two dozen pieces before being transported on sledges to St. Petersburg.

"I could smell the animal. In the end, all my clothes smelt of him. It was wonderful."
Bernard Buigues

Swedish geophysicist Per Wikstrom uses ground radar to scan the permafrost where Jarkov's tusks and head were found.

First, Buigues had to make sure there really was a mammoth carcass in the permafrost. He returned later that year with a Swedish geophysicist who scanned the spot with ground-penetrating radar that can "see" objects under the earth. The data indicated that all or most of the mammoth was buried 15 ft (4.6 m) below ground. Now, all Buigues had to do was come up with a strategy for removing the 6.75-ton (6.1-t) corpse intact and transporting it, still frozen, across 200 mi (320 km) of roadless tundra to Khatanga.

It would be a major operation, involving experts who had experience of excavating and preserving mammoth remains. The cost would run into millions of dollars—in the end, much of the necessary money was put up by America's Discovery Channel and the French magazine Paris Match.

Spring 1999—Assembling the experts

As news of the exciting discovery spread, scientists from around the world offered to join the excavation. A dozen research projects were submitted, and 25 scientists volunteered to take part in the detailed examination of the mammoth. By the spring of 1999, Buigues had assembled a recovery team that included mammoth experts and paleontologists from France, Russia, the United States, and the Netherlands.

Meanwhile, researchers had been busy examining the remains Buigues had already recovered. The size and shape of the tusks confirmed that the mammoth was a large male; female mammoth tusks are much smaller, partly because they stop growing when the animal is suckling young. Radiocarbon dating of the tusks and bones revealed that this specimen died 20,380 years ago, around the time of the glaciers of the last ice age. Analysis of the mammoth's teeth indicated that he was about 47 when he died.

In recognition of the family that brought this creature to light, Buigues named him Jarkov.

Dental records

Experts were able to tell how old Jarkov was when he died by examining his teeth. Like modern elephants, mammoths had two big molars in the top jaw and two in the bottom jaw. The teeth were replaced five times during a mammoth's life, with new sets taking the place of worn teeth in a kind of conveyor belt system. The tiny baby teeth lasted only about 18 months, then they were replaced by another set, lasting until about six years of age.

The final set appeared when the mammoth was about 40 years old. These molars measured an astonishing 12 in (30 cm) by 10 in (25 cm). Only about 1 in (2.5 cm) of the tooth projected above the gum, but the buried portion pushed up to compensate for wear. Eventually, though, there would be no chewing surface left, and then the mammoth would slowly starve to death. This simple fact probably meant that very few mammoths lived much longer than 60 to 70 years.

September 20, 1999—The frozen North

Two years after Simion Jarkov found the mammoth that bears his name, the expedition finally got under way. On September 20, part of the team flew from Moscow to join Buigues, the expedition leader, at the excavation site on Siberia's Taimyr Peninsula.

Jutting into the Arctic Ocean, Taimyr is 3,000 mi (4,800 km) and three time zones away from the Russian capital. The region is larger than France or Texas. In every direction, the land stretches away in a gray-green wilderness of treeless swamp and snow-streaked tundra dotted with lakes and crisscrossed by rivers. Even in September, ice gleams on the lakes.

On board the plane is scientist Larry Agenbroad, professor of geology at Northern Arizona University. One of the world's leading mammoth specialists, Agenbroad is director of the Hot Springs Mammoth Site in South Dakota, the largest concentration of Columbian mammoth skeletons in the world. After examining bones and droppings for 30 years, Agenbroad is excited by the possibility of seeing, touching, and smelling a woolly mammoth in the flesh, a prospect he describes as "the frosting on the cake of my career."

Scientists wearing sterile suits and face masks prepare to remove cell tissue from Jarkov's jaw. Some researchers hope that DNA extracted from undamaged cells can be used to clone a mammoth.

Cell tissue samples are bagged before being sent for laboratory analysis. Research institutes in Europe, Japan, and the United States are involved in the quest to extract DNA from Jarkov.

21

DIARY OF THE EXPEDITION

Dutch scientist Dick Mol examines strands of Jarkov's hair exposed at the surface of the block. Mol hopes that Jarkov's coat will tell researchers a lot more about how woolly mammoths were adapted to the cold.

Dressed in sterile clothing to avoid contaminating the sample, a scientist removes some of Jarkov's hair. Pollen trapped in the mammoth's coat could tell us more about the vegetation that grew in Siberia when he was alive.

A magnifying glass shows the wiry texture of the hairs on Jarkov's outer coat. Beneath this was a layer of thick fur. It is possible that woolly mammoths molted, shedding their coats each spring as warmer weather arrived.

atmosphere is very friendly. Agenbroad is impressed by the fact that he never hears anyone swearing.

Although there are few entertainments on-site, there is plenty to think about. One of the many mysteries about woolly mammoths is how they found enough to eat in a region as far north as Taimyr, where the growing season lasts only a few months and the vegetation is stunted and meager. Nowadays, the largest herbivores in Siberia are reindeer, which eat mainly moss and lichen. The stomach contents of frozen mammoths show that they enjoyed a much richer and more varied diet. If a cloned mammoth were released on the Taimyr Peninsula today, it would soon starve to death. So, if the tundra wouldn't support mammoths during the current period of

global warming, how did they survive this far north when the climate was so much colder than it is now?

The answer, according to the experts, is that the Ice Age climate wasn't just cold. It was also very dry. Even today, the polar regions are the driest on Earth, with the South Pole receiving less precipitation than the

Sahara Desert. During the Ice Age, probably only a few inches of rain and snow fell on the Taimyr Peninsula each year. The snow cover quickly melted in the summer, and the permafrost thawed to a much greater depth than it does today. As a result, the soil supported grasses, herbs, and sagebrush, with groups of birch and larch trees in sheltered pockets.

This "mammoth steppe" stretched right across Eurasia from the Arctic Ocean to the Black Sea. Pollen recovered from Jarkov's hair indicates that he lived on the mammoth steppe. Besides being remarkably tough, capable of remaining intact for millions of years, pollen grains have distinctive surface patterns. Identifying the pollen found on Jarkov will help scientists build a picture of what plants grew in Taimyr more than 20,000 years ago. In turn, that will provide clues to the climate in Siberia during the last ice age.

Pollen profiles can be misleading, though. For example, if researchers find a lot of pine pollen on Jarkov, it won't necessarily mean that he lived in a pine forest—or anywhere near one. Pine trees produce more pollen than most trees, and the grains are so light that they can be carried by the wind hundreds of miles from their source.

If Jarkov's internal organs are preserved, the contents of his stomach and large intestine will be analyzed to find out what he ate.

September 29—Differences of opinion

A week after the start of the excavation, the team still hasn't got a jackhammer. Two more scientists have joined the expedition. Yves Coppens, a French paleontologist, was a member of the team that identified the skeleton of "Lucy," a female hominid who lived in Africa more than three million years ago. Alexei Tikhonov, an expert on the woolly mammoth, is chairman of the Mammoth Committee of the Russian Academy of Sciences.

Buigues has brought Jarkov's tusks to the site. One of them weighs 97 lb (44 kg), and the other tips the scales at 103 lb (47 kg). That is average for a male woolly mammoth tusk; the largest ever found weighed 185 lb (84 kg). Even after 20,000 years underground, they show few signs of deterioration. They still bear the flattened areas on the outside curves where they were worn down by scrubbing away snow. On some tusks, the wear patterns are more marked on one tusk

Each of the five tents, heated by a stove, slept five people. They ate reindeer and fish supplied by local Dolgans. All other supplies had to be flown in from Khatanga, more than 200 mi (320 km) away.

By working out how Jarkov is lying in the ground, Buigues and the team hope to remove the mammoth undamaged from the permafrost.

than on the other, showing that mammoths were "right-tusked" or "left-tusked," similar to people being right- or left-handed.

Buigues arranges the tusks on the grave in the same position they were in when the Jarkov brothers found them. From the position of the tusks and Buigues's description of how the head was located, the scientists try to work out how the rest of the body might be lying. The team is anxious to avoid any possibility of damaging the mammoth as they dig deeper, and they want to keep the block as small as possible.

There are differences of opinion among the expedition members about how much of Jarkov actually remains inside the block. Buigues is hopeful that 85 to 90 percent of the mammoth has been preserved. Mol is more cautious, predicting that most of the rear end and midsection of the carcass could be recovered. Tikhonov believes there's a good chance that the object detected by the ground radar in 1998 was not a mammoth but a large mass of ice. He

"The quality of the tusks was so fresh that it looked like the mammoth was living yesterday, and when I rubbed my hand across the thick layers of warm fur, it was like touching a furry, live animal."

Dick Mol

predicts that when the block is thawed, only about one-third of Jarkov's bones, plus fragments of skin and hair, will be found.

The team members also disagree on the cloning issue. The question is not so much whether it is possible to recreate the woolly mammoth; everybody agrees that the chances of cloning a mammoth are small. Instead, the discussion focuses on whether it would be right to bring an extinct animal back to life.

Dick Mol, while admitting that he would be "thrilled" to see mammoths roaming the earth again, thinks that cloning them is a "crazy idea." He believes that mammoths were wiped out by habitat destruction due to climate change. To release mammoths into a world that no longer contains their Ice Age habitat would be a crime against nature. He also points out that mammoths were social animals, which possibly traveled in herds up to 30 strong. A single cloned mammoth would be condemned to live out a lonely existence in a zoo.

After a hard day's digging, workers return to camp. In the early days the team used picks and shovels.

Dwarf mammoths

In 1993, scientists who believed that mammoths were wiped out by climatic warming received a jolt. Russian researchers announced that they had found the remains of mammoths that had lived 7,000 years after the last ice age ended. The youngest remains were only 3,700 years old, which means that the animals were living after the first Egyptian pyramids were built.

The mammoths were discovered on Wrangel Island (see page 11), 125 mi (200 km) north of eastern Siberia. After the ice sheets melted and sea levels rose, the mammoths were cut off from the mainland. Over the thousands of years that they remained isolated, the mammoths evolved into a dwarf race, growing only 6 ft (1.8 m) tall. The Wrangel Island mammoths disappeared around the period that humans reached their lonely preserve. Their survival into historical times strengthens the arguments of scientists who believe that they were wiped out by humans. If humans killed off the mammoths, there may be moral grounds for using cloning techniques to bring them back to life.

As the trenches around Jarkov get deeper, Buigues calculates how to reduce the weight of the block. It weighs about 6 tons (5.4 t) more than is safe for the helicopter that will fly and carry it to Khatanga.

September 30—Heavy load

Conditions are perfect, with sunny skies and a hard frost. Buigues has got hold of two jackhammers, but when the diggers try to use them, they discover that the generator isn't powerful enough. While Buigues makes another trip to Khatanga to get a more powerful generator, the rest of the team continue digging the trenches with hand tools. Two sides of the mammoth block are composed mainly of ice, which can be chipped away with pickaxes and shovels.

Buigues and the scientists have thought about how to recover the mammoth without damaging it. The plan sounds straightforward—dig trenches all around Jarkov, drill holes beneath him, slide iron bars through the holes, weld the bars together, place a sling under the reinforced block, and then lift the entire mass clear with a helicopter.

Easier said than done. The mammoth and its permafrost coffin could weigh as much as 29 tons (26.1 t). That's equivalent to the weight of 330 adult humans, a load that would almost fill a jumbo jet. But Jarkov and his frozen tomb won't be flown to Khatanga stowed securely in the hold of an airliner. He will be carried the 200 mi (320 km) dangling in a harness.

The Jarkov family who found the mammoth sometimes visit the camp on reindeer sled or on foot, searching for domesticated reindeer that have wandered off with a wild herd. They watch the team's efforts with some amusement, wondering why anybody would waste so much time digging out an object that has no practical value.

October 4—Getting somewhere

At last, a generator powerful enough to run the compressor has been delivered to the site by helicopter. Armed with a pair of jackhammers that work, the excavation team makes rapid progress. The trenches get deeper by the hour, and it looks as if the job will be finished within a week.

Two days later, the trenches are more than 6 ft (1.8 m) deep, and the block containing Jarkov has been hacked into its rough final shape. Now only its base is attached to the earth.

The helicopter that will transport Jarkov to Khatanga is a Mil MI-26 model, the largest non-military helicopter in the world, designed to carry a 22.5-ton (20.3-t) load. There's just one problem. The block containing Jarkov is estimated to weigh 29 tons (26.1 t). Some of this excess baggage will have to be shaved off.

During the dig, Dolgans have visited the site to report more mammoth finds. Buigues says he knows of another 18 locations containing Ice Age relics—not only mammoths, but also woolly rhinos, steppe lions, and giant elk. He hopes to excavate these specimens and put them on display in a cold museum that the Russians are planning to create in Khatanga.

Buigues is not the only person on the trail of extinct Ice Age mammals. A Japanese team has plans to stock a "Pleistocene Park" in eastern Siberia with cloned mammoths and saber-toothed cats. Akira Ititani, a geneticist in Japan, predicts that mammoths will be roaming in this sanctuary within 20 years. He and his colleagues are offering $9,000 for samples of mammoth tissue suitable for cloning experiments. Competition for well-preserved remains is fierce. There is even a rumor that some Dolgans have been offered villas in the south of France in exchange for supplying valuable finds.

Mammoths are definitely becoming big business. During the operation to recover Jarkov, an American on-line auction firm was preparing to sell an incomplete Siberian mammoth skeleton called Mambo. They set a starting price of $115,000, with hopes that a bidding war could push the price up to

> **"Even if DNA in body cells [is] degraded, sperm DNA may be fine. If sperm chromosomes are intact, we may be able to produce a mammoth-elephant hybrid."**
>
> Dr Ryuzo Yanagimachi, scientist

$500,000. In January 2000, a single Alaskan mammoth tusk was auctioned for $34,500, while a Siberian mammoth tusk made more than $12,000 at the same sale. With so much money at stake, Buigues fears that the Russian mafia could muscle in on the mammoth trade.

As the excavation nears completion, a Russian workman uses a jackhammer to drill holes through the base of the block. Iron bars were then slid through the holes to provide a support for the block.

October 11—Hit by storms

Hopes that the dig would have been completed by now have been dashed by the weather. On October 7, the camp was hit by a gale, which whipped up a furious ground blizzard. Since then, it has snowed every day. Each morning, the digging crew members have to spend valuable time shoveling snow out of the trenches. The team has tried to protect the site by rigging a piece of canvas over it.

The weather isn't the only cause for concern. Although Buigues has been building up a stock of aviation fuel, there isn't enough to keep the giant helicopter in the air for its 400-mi (650-km) round-trip from Khatanga. If he can't persuade the airport officials to supply extra kerosene, Jarkov could be stranded in his pit until next year.

As the workers prepare to put a platform under Jarkov, they notice a foul smell and discover green plant matter in the ground at the bottom of the

> "For the first time a frozen Pleistocene animal has been carefully removed from the permafrost as a complete animal, and placed in a controlled atmosphere where it can be studied."
>
> Larry Agenbroad

Protected from the snow by a makeshift tent, Buigues dries a piece of Jarkov's woolly coat. Mol said the hair's pungent smell reminded him of the odor of the elephant house in the zoo.

A Russian workman welds together the frame that will hold Jarkov on his flight to Khatanga. Once the frame was in place, the block was freed from the permafrost by drilling away the ice between the rods supporting the base.

The night sky over the camp is lit by the ghostly glow of the aurora borealis, or "northern lights." The aurora is produced when gases in the upper atmosphere are bombarded by solar particles attracted toward the earth's magnetic poles.

trench. Mol thinks this is the remains of ancient swamp vegetation. The discovery raises the possibility that Jarkov died after becoming trapped in a bog.

Many people assume that the best-preserved mammoths are those that died during the coldest part of the last ice age—between about 30,000 to 14,000 years ago. In fact, Jarkov is the only mammoth containing soft tissue that dates from this period. All the other specimens of similar age are only skeletons. Scientists think these mammoths died in such cold and dry conditions that their bodies remained on the surface of the tundra, where their flesh rotted away or was eaten by scavengers.

Mammoth remains with flesh still attached lived either much earlier or later than Jarkov. For example, baby Dima and the Beresovka mammoth died between 30,000 and 40,000 years ago, when the climate was relatively warm and wet (see pages 14–15). Scientists think that these animals fell into bogs or were swept away by summer floods, and then froze during the following winter.

October 17—Lift-off!

A week of bad weather, and the skies have cleared. The canvas sheet didn't stop snow from getting into the trenches, so yesterday it was replaced by an inflatable tent. Under this, the digging crew finished isolating the block. They inserted steel bars into holes drilled under the block, and then chiseled away the remaining sections of permafrost with jackhammers. Now the block rests on the platform waiting for the airlift.

For dramatic effect, Buigues has fixed the tusks onto the block so that the mammoth appears to be bursting out of his grave. "For me this mammoth is a star," Buigues explains. "I had to take care of him like a star. To travel from [the] place where he slept for more than 20,000 years without his tusks was a pity. I wanted to give him a second life."

Word reaches the camp that the airlift is to go ahead today. The helicopter will reach the site in two hours. While some of the team hastily dismantles the camp, the crew responsible for loading the block checks the harness of 3-in-(8-cm) thick cables that will be attached to the helicopter's lifting gear.

The helicopter approaches out of a clear sky. As it flies over the camp, the downdraft from its 100-ft (30-m) diameter blades sends a tent and other gear blowing across the site. The pilot lands several hundred yards away and strolls over to assess the scale of the task. Deciding that his huge machine can tackle the job, he takes off and puts the helicopter into a hover above Jarkov. On the ground, buffeted by the gale from above, the Russian workers struggle to attach the harness to the lifting gear.

At last the ground crew signals that the harness is fixed. The helicopter begins to rise. Even on full power, it can barely cope with the 26-ton (23.4-t) load. There are anxious gasps from the spectators as the block containing Jarkov scrapes along the ground. After being dragged about 150 ft (45.7 m), the load rises clear, and the helicopter climbs into the sky.

Two hours later, Jarkov is standing on the runway at Khatanga airport, surrounded by jubilant expedition members. The block will stay here until the following spring, and then it will be moved into the ice cave, ready for examination by scientists.

With the helicopter standing by, Buigues takes a last look at Jarkov and his recently added tusks—"I wanted him to arrive complete at his new home," he explained.

"My heart was in my mouth because at first, the helicopter couldn't lift off, and it dragged the carcass across the snow for about 50 yards."

Bernard Buigues

Dangling beneath a giant Mil MI-26 helicopter, Jarkov sets off on his flight to Khatanga. After spending the winter at the town's airport, the block was moved into an ice cave for detailed scientific examination.

Examining Jarkov

The permafrost block containing Jarkov spent the winter wrapped in a tarpaulin beside the runway at Khatanga airport. It turned out that the giant trophy was too big to fit through the entrance to the ice cave. In early 2000, Buigues returned to enlarge the opening, and Jarkov was finally moved into the cold, frozen cave at the end of March.

To protect the mammoth from contamination, a laboratory was constructed around the block. Here, scientists from several countries will spend a year examining Jarkov in detail. Working in subzero conditions, they will use hair dryers to defrost Jarkov hair by hair. As tissue and other remains are exposed, samples will be collected and sent for analysis to research institutions around the world.

Some results have already been obtained. Ice taken from the block around Jarkov has been matched with samples collected from an ancient ice cap in the north of Taimyr. By comparing the chemical composition of the ice samples, scientists have dated the ice in the block and established that it is the same age as Jarkov himself— about 20,000 years old. This is great news for the scientists who will be studying pollen and insect samples to reconstruct the vegetation and climate of Jarkov's habitat.

Buigues has also sent samples of mammoth tissue to a laboratory for possible attempts to clone the animal, but he admits it may be many decades before his ambition to bring back the woolly mammoth is achieved. He is also cautious about what will be revealed as the block is

tusks

hair

tissue

teeth

thawed. "We don't expect to find red flesh, but rather a kind of dried meat," he said.

Mol also plays down expectations, but he thinks that Jarkov could be a gold mine for mammoth researchers. Hair samples from different parts of his body could help scientists reconstruct the mammoth coat in detail. The hairs may reveal whether mammoths molted.

The mystery of how much of Jarkov has been preserved should be solved when scientists use a machine called an X-ray tomographer to scan the contents of the block. Tomographers, which are used in brain scans, take detailed X-ray photographs of thin "slices" of tissue. By taking hundreds of photographs and piecing them together by computer, scientists should be able to obtain a 3-D picture of Jarkov.

If the results show that Jarkov's intestines are intact and still contain food, Larry Agenbroad hopes to compare the diet of Siberian woolly mammoths with the diet of Columbian mammoths in North America.

Ross MacPhee is another American scientist who will be taking part in the examination. MacPhee, a curator at the American Museum of Natural History in New York, believes that mammoths were wiped out by a disease introduced by humans. In search of evidence for this "hyper-disease" scenario, MacPhee hopes to recover genetic material from Jarkov's bones and tissue that could reveal the presence of infectious disease causing microbes such as bacteria and viruses.

"This is the closest I'll probably get to touching and seeing the animal, or the kissing cousin of the animal, that I've been pursuing all my life."

Larry Agenbroad

Mol believes that the Jarkov project marks the beginning of a new era in mammoth research. Now that scientists have pioneered a successful technique for excavating a huge frozen animal and transporting it to safe storage, Mol thinks that many more researchers will come to Taimyr in search of Ice Age mammals. Although the Dolgans are not sure what all the fuss is about, the knowledge that mammoths are valuable not only for their tusks could result in many more specimens being recovered intact.

For Agenbroad, the Jarkov project has been a refreshing cultural experience as well as a great scientific achievement. "It was wonderful," he says, "all of us there working for a common goal." Buigues, whose vision and persistence turned a dream into reality, also sees the mammoth as a symbol linking people of different countries and cultures. The remote Siberian town of Khatanga is now twinned with the French village of Rouffignac, the site of a cave containing many mammoth Ice Age drawings and engravings.

Meeting Jarkov

As soon as I walked into the cave I was overwhelmed. Although the cave itself was dimly lit, the walls and ceiling sparkled with frost. The floor was solid ice, forcing me to shuffle along slowly. After two or three minutes I rounded the corner and came face-to-face with the mammoth.

Although the block of ice was still unthawed, I could clearly see the mammoth's hair protruding from the top of the block. I climbed up on top and touched it. It felt just like modern-day elephant's hair, which I wasn't expecting. The color was different, but the feel of it was so natural. It turned my perception of the mammoth from "museum exhibit" to "animal frozen in time" in an instant.

However, the most fantastic part was the tusks. They were quite large, with a beautiful curve to them. As I ran my hands along their length, eyes closed, I could easily imagine this animal was alive.

> **"The sensation was no different from running my hands along the tusks of a living, breathing bull elephant."**

The smoothness of the tusks was astounding. As well as the texture, the way they changed from off-white to a yellowish color near the base is exactly like the elephants that I work with. I found it almost unreal that this magnificent creature came to an end over 20,000 years before I met him. All in all a humbling experience.

Ryan Hockley, Elephant Keeper
Longleat Safari Park, U.K.
from the Khatanga ice cave, June 2000

Could mammoths live again?

Jarkov will thaw into a world where science leaps ahead almost daily. Clones like Dolly the sheep, in the UK, make world news. Eggs and sperm of animals and people are deep-frozen to make babies later. Can science bring Jarkov or his kind back to life?

Dolly the sheep was an identical genetic copy of another sheep—in effect, her much older twin sister.

The hybrid method

If Jarkov's sex organs are well preserved, they may contain frozen male sex cells—sperm. Using "test tube baby" techniques, or artificial insemination, as in farm animals, his sperm could be joined with eggs. There are no existing mammoth eggs, but those from a close living relative, say, the Asian elephant, might work. Jarkov would be the father, the female elephant the mother. The baby would grow in her womb and be a hybrid—half-mammoth, half-elephant. If this were done several times, long-term breeding among the offspring might eventually produce creatures similar to mammoths.

The cloning method

Clones are living things with exactly the same genes (genetic instructions). But being clones does not make two animals exactly the same. In scientific terms, identical twins are clones. But they soon grow to look and behave differently.

Cloning requires genes, and these are made of genetic material, DNA. Suppose DNA can be obtained from Jarkov's sperm, blood, or bone marrow. Take a suitable cell, probably an Asian elephant egg cell, remove its DNA, and put in Jarkov's mammoth DNA. The egg then uses this new or implanted DNA for genetic instructions and develops into a baby mammoth.

Too many problems?

Both methods overflow with problems, however. For sperm to thaw undamaged, they must be deep-frozen fast and kept very cold. Similarly, a temperature rise, even to $-4°F$ ($-20°C$), breaks up DNA and makes it useless for cloning. Scientists tried to obtain DNA from well-frozen animals such as the 1978 Khatanga mammoth. But far too much was missing, and the pieces left had smashed into tiny bits.

Which is Jarkov's closest living relative—the African elephant (*left*) or the Asian elephant (*right*)?

"A lot of people ask: 'Why clone?' I say 'Why not?' This is an animal that was hunted to extinction by man. It's almost as if we have a moral obligation to bring it back."

Larry Agenbroad

Should we?

Jarkov in his block of ice may reveal scientific evidence about his life and times. Also, even a few fragments of DNA might help to find out who the woolly mammoth's closest living relative is—the Asian or the African elephant. His body and tissues could be preserved, so that he might be bred or cloned in the future. But even if we could bring mammoths back to life—should we?

Finding out more

MUSEUMS

American Museum of Natural History, New York
http://www.amnh.org
Skeleton of mammoth, mummified remains of a baby woolly mammoth

Denver Museum of Nature & Science, Colorado
http://www.dmnh.org
Columbian mammoth skeletons and skulls

Field Museum of Natural History, Chicago
http://www.fmnh.org
Mammoth bones and bone hut

Florida Museum of Natural History, Gainesville, Florida
http://www.flmnh.ufl.edu
Columbian and ancestral mammoths

Illinois State Museum, Springfield
http://www.museum.state.il.us
Mammoth bones, teeth, and hair

Mammoth Site of Hot Springs
http://www.mammothsite.com
Woolly and Columbian mammoth remains; center covers an Ice Age sinkhole that trapped hundreds of mammoths 26,000 years ago

National Museum of Natural History, Washington, DC
http://www.nmnh.si.edu
Many fossils from the ice ages

Natural History Museum of Los Angeles County, California
http://www.nhm.org
Rancho La Brea Tar Pits; Columbian mammoth skeleton and life-size models

University of Nebraska State Museum, Lincoln
http://www.museum.unl.edu/
Columbian mammoth skeleton

BIBLIOGRAPHY

Lister, Adrian and Bahn, Paul. *Mammoths*. Boxtree, 1995. (History of the origin of mammoths, their lives, and eventual extinction.)

Ward, Peter. *The Call of Distant Mammoths*. Copernicus, 1997. (A scientific and detailed look at the possible reasons why mammoths disappeared from North America, along with other large mammals.)

WEB SITES

Raising the Mammoth
http://www.discovery.com/exp/mammoth/mammoth.html
Discovery Online site giving the full story of the Jarkov project. Packed with pictures and interactive features, with links to other mammoth Web sites

The Mammoth Story
http://rbcm1.rbcm.gov.bc.ca/discover/ds24295/index_fs.html
Good introduction to mammoth natural history

Mammuthus: The Migration Will Begin
http://www.mammuthus.com/
An interesting account of mammoth evolution and lifestyle

All About Mammoths
http://www.zoomwhales.com/subjects/mammals/mammoth/
Enchanted Learning Web site featuring woolly mammoths and other Ice Age animals

What Killed the Mammoth?
http://sciencebulletins.amnh.org/biobulletin/biobulletin/story984.html
American Museum of Natural History Web site on the extinction of the mammoths

The Mammoths' Demise
http://www.discoveringarchaeology.com/0599toc/5cover1-mammoth.shtml
Another, more detailed, account of mammoth extinctions, with links to articles by scientists discussing the different possible causes—overhunting, climate change, and disease

Open Season on the Woolly Mammoth
http://www.nwf.org/nwf/intlwild/mammoth.html
Interesting *International Wildlife Magazine* article on the trade in Russian mammoth ivory

Mammoth sites and finds

1 Ahlen, Germany
Woolly mammoth skeleton, mounted in Münster Museum

2 Angus, Nebraska, U.S.A.
Mammoth skeleton found early 1900s, probably a variety of Columbian mammoth

3 Aucilla River, Florida, U.S.A.
Silt in bottom of river containing Columbian mammoth skeletons

4 Azov, southern Russia
Steppe mammoth skeleton nearly 15 ft (4.5 m) high excavated and mounted

5 Berelekh, northeastern Siberia
Most northern Paleolithic site in the world containing thousands of mammoth bones

6 Beresovka, northeastern Siberia
Well-preserved frozen mammoth excavated in 1901; the skeleton and stuffed hide now in St. Petersburg, Russia (see page 14)

7 Big Bone Lick, Kentucky, U.S.A.
Salt bog yielding some of the latest Columbian mammoth remains in America

8 Blackwater Draw, New Mexico, U.S.A.
Mammoth remains

9 Clovis, New Mexico, U.S.A.
Originally a spring-fed pond where mammoths found; a Blackwater Draw site (see 8 above)

10 Colby, Wyoming, U.S.A.
Parts of Columbian mammoths stacked together

11 Elephant Point, Eschscholtz Bay, Alaska, U.S.A.
First reported mammoth carcass find in Alaska, made in 1907

12 Fairbanks Creek, Alaska, U.S.A.
Face, trunk, and foreleg of calf found in 1948

13 Franklin County, Nebraska, U.S.A.
Columbian mammoth skull found in 1915, now displayed at the University of Nebraska Museum

14 Hay Springs, Nebraska, U.S.A.
Remains of early Columbian mammoths

15 Heilongjiang, Zhaoyuan, Shan Zhan, Harbin, China
Most complete woolly mammoth skeleton found in China

16 Hot Springs, South Dakota, U.S.A.
About 50 Columbian mammoth skeleton remains in a sinkhole

17 Jonesboro, Indiana, U.S.A.
Columbian mammoth skeleton found in 1903, mounted in American Museum of Natural History, New York

18 Khatanga, Siberia
Frozen mammoth carcass found in 1977, dated to more than 45,000 years ago

19 Kirgilyakh, Siberia
Baby Dima, mammoth discovered in 1977 (see page 15)

20 Lehner Ranch, Arizona, U.S.A.
13 young Columbian mammoths

21 Lena, Siberia
Adams mammoth's frozen carcass discovered in 1799 (see page 14)

22 Liakhov Islands, Siberia
Small male adult mammoth found in 1901, skeleton donated to Muséum Nationale d'Histoire Naturelle, Paris

23 Nogaisk, southern Russian Federation
Ancestral mammoth skeleton, mounted in the Zoological Museum in St. Petersburg, Russia

24 Rancho La Brea, Los Angeles, California, U.S.A.
Columbian mammoths who met their deaths caught in tar seeps

25 Sevsk, Russian Federation
Mammoth cemetery, biggest find in Europe; seven almost intact skeletons including three babies

26 Taimyr, Siberia
Almost complete woolly mammoth skeleton found in 1948, which has become the type specimen for this species

27 Trinity River, Dallas, Texas, U.S.A.
Many Columbian

mammoth remains found in sand and gravel pits since the 1920s

28 Wellsch Valley, Saskatchewan, Canada
Some of earliest ancestral mammoth remains in North America—about $1^{1}/_{2}$ million years old

29 Wrangel Island, northeastern Siberia
Dwarf woolly mammoths found; only 7,000–3,700 years old (see page 27)

30 Yamal Peninsula, Siberia
1988 baby mammoth Mascha, westernmost Siberian frozen carcass found

Index